I0119225

Simon Fitz Simons

An essay in refutation of agnosticism and the philosophy of

the unknowable

A review with an analogy

Simon Fitz Simons

An essay in refutation of agnosticism and the philosophy of the unknowable
A review with an analogy

ISBN/EAN: 9783337221805

Printed in Europe, USA, Canada, Australia, Japan

Cover: Foto ©Andreas Hilbeck / pixelio.de

More available books at **www.hansebooks.com**

AN ESSAY

IN

REFUTATION OF AGNOSTICISM

AND

THE PHILOSOPHY OF THE UNKNOWABLE.

A REVIEW WITH AN ANALOGY.

BY

REV. SIMON FITZ SIMONS.

PRICE 25 CENTS.

ROCHESTER, N. Y.:
POST-EXPRESS PRINTING COMPANY,
1889.

PREFACE.

ERRATA.

	PAGE.	LINE.
Supply (1) reference for foot-note before irreligion,	25	4
For omnipotent read omnipresent	27	9
For sunset read sunshine,	44	19
Supply quotation mark (") before " be those negations," at beginning of line.	45	13
Supply quotation mark (") before demonstrable.	45	15
Supply quotation (') before duty at beginning of line, and quotation mark (') before interrogation point at close of sentence,	54	20
For legitimate read illegitimate,	55	5

POSTSCRIPT.

For arcs read sides,	73	25

(which, in the mouth of an agnostic has, with a more decided dogmatism and more magisterial air, usurped the place of the long familiar and harmless editorial *we*). Should the reader find them offensive, the apology must be that both have been deliberately borrowed from the agnostic school.

PREFACE.

This is a very small book to challenge the attention of a great public, but nowadays brevity in book-making seems to be a virtue rather than a defect, and the tract or pamphlet which may be read through in a half-hour is apt to find more readers than the ponderous and learned volume which demands leisure and close study.

The following pages were written at the close of the Agnostic Controversy which was waged beyond the Atlantic during the first six months of the present year, and were originally intended for magazine publication. The consideration, however, that their circulation would thus be limited by the subscription list of a magazine, suggested an independent publication in the present form.

The tone advisedly adopted for the magazine has been retained, as also has been the personal pronoun, first person singular, (which, in the mouth of an agnostic has, with a more decided dogmatism and more magisterial air, usurped the place of the long familiar and harmless editorial *we*). Should the reader find them offensive, the apology must be that both have been deliberately borrowed from the agnostic school.

Regarding the argument it may be briefly mentioned that Christian apologetics, intent only on defence, have lately for the most part been exercised in merely parrying the thrusts of agnostics, and have seldom undertaken to carry the war into the enemy's camp, and that agnostics, as if keenly alive to the weakness of their own position, had seemed determined to keep the public gaze averted from their own weak defences by unceasingly calling attention to what they chose to call weak points in Christianity. As agnosticism asserted nothing positive, and contented itself with merely denying, it was quite natural that the apologist of revealed religion should never dream of examining a simple negation or mere denial. Yet there must be a reason for denial as well as for affirmation, a justification for saying "No" as well as for saying "Yes;" and in point of fact agnosticism has given a reason for its negations and denials. It is with this reason the argument of this little tract deals. It is to be regretted that some one better equipped for the task has not undertaken it. I have done little else than point out the fallacy in the agnostic position, and indeed nothing further is required for its refutation. How far I have succeded in cutting from beneath agnostic feet the ground on which they stand the unbiased reader will determine for himself.   S. F.

A REFUTATION OF AGNOSTICISM.

AGNOSTICISM AND THE UNKNOWABLE;
A REVIEW WITH AN ANALOGY.

A protracted discussion has been carried on in the pages of the *Nineteenth Century* during the greater part of the present year of grace on the respective merits of Agnosticism and Christianity. It was waged between Professor Huxley on the one hand and Professor Wace on the other, and ended, as such discussions usually do, without much additional light being thrown upon either side of the subject. Professor Wace, it must be admitted, made a noble plea for his side, but nowhere does he go to the bottom of the subject or strike a blow at the root of agnosticism. His argument is defensive. Nor has any one, so far as I have seen, chosen to examine the merits of agnosticism unless it be the agnostic Frederic Harrison—

agnostic, positivist, and Comtist. And yet agnosticism is the present fashionable foible of irreligion. In the closing years of this 19th century it seems to be the form which infidelity is assuming.

I propose, therefore, to examine the validity of the agnostic position, and by a very simple analogy to show that a position which has been regarded as impregnable, inasmuch as it is negative, is quite the reverse. My appeal will be to the sober reason of men of thought, believing that for the most part men are willing to admit the force of argument when neither prejudice nor bias stands in the way. With those who hold a brief for agnosticism and the Unknowable, of course argument is vain, and to men who will cavil at the most palpable truth, the argument is not addressed. Professor Huxley proclaims himself the father of agnosticism, and of course it would be cruel and cowardly in him to abandon his offspring, and Mr.

Spencer holds a similar relation to the Unknowable. Moreover, the analogy which I shall use is so simple, but at the same time so aptly fitted to the situation of the Unknowable and its religion, agnosticism, that agnostic Goliaths are apt to despise and deride it as a mere pebble from the brook.

What is Agnosticism?

First of all, however, it is necessary to come to a right understanding of what agnosticism really is ; and this is by no means an easy task. Agnosticism is anything but an unchangeable quantity, and and day by day it is becoming more and more an unsteady factor, with a tendency to branch off into as many agnostic sects as there are agnostic individuals. Professor Huxley himself is keenly alive to these deplorable divisions in the household of agnostic faith, and evidently regards his followers as in a state of hopeless insubordination, for his latest utterances are notably marked by such

parenthetic explanations as "agnostic principles (as I draw them)";
"agnosticism (*me judice*)"; "speaking for myself," etc., evidencing Mr.
Huxley's despair over this hopeless
disunion if not disorganization.
There are, however,

Three Marked Authorities

who have undertaken to expound
agnosticism to the world, and, as
far as I am aware, 'only three, and
each of these in turn I shall notice
briefly. The latest variation is that
of Mr. Laing. Before and after him
is Professor Huxley, and prior to
both Mr. Herbert Spencer.

A brief notice will suffice for the

Agnosticism of Mr. Laing,

and if I seem to dismiss him rather
summarily, it will be seen that I

---

1 It would be an obvious absurdity to class Col.
Ingersoll with these exponents of agnosticism. No
thinking man has ever claimed for him recognition
as a scientist, a philosopher, or a man of deep
thought. Indeed, in his late agnostic utterances
against revealed religion it is doubtful whether he
has not helped rather than injured the cause of
Christianity by his application of the brutal method
of the lawyer brow-beating the witness. Besides
the world no longer takes him seriously.

merely follow illustrious precedent.
The story runneth thus: Professor
Huxley claims, with some showing
of justice, the rather dubious distinction of being the real inventor
of agnosticism. He wishes to be regarded as its father and founder.
He claims to have given it a name
and distinction, and possibly an
abiding place among the many and
varied *isms* that afflict poor human-
ity. The demon of schism, however, seems to have crept into the
agnostic fold. In an evil hour Mr.
Gladstone flung in the apple of dis-
cord. It would appear that ignoring or not not knowing the rightful
seat of agnostic authority, "Mr.
Gladstone[1] (as Professor Huxley
relates it) asked Mr. Laing if he
could draw up a short summary
of the negative creed," and to the
infinite disgust of Professor Huxley and without seal or sanction
of his, "Mr. Laing at once," the professor tells us with cold, biting

[1] *Nineteenth Century*, February, 1889.

irony, "kindly obliged Mr. Gladstone with the desired articles— eight of them," he adds with undisguised contempt. Professor Huxley tells us he patiently read over the "eight articles" until he "met with polarity in Article viii.," when, happily bethinking him of the scriptural injunction to "suffer fools gladly," he refrained with wonderful self-mastery from anathematizing and excommunicating Mr. Laing, and was simply content to "shut the book" in a manner which, if not minatory, was surely highly damnatory. He rejects Mr. Laing's "eight articles" *in toto*, ridicules his pretensions, and, with a deep sense of outraged authority, proceeds to tell the world what he would have said "if anyone had preferred the request to him"—the legitimate authority on the subject. He takes occasion to clearly define his authority as Supreme Pontiff; plainly sets forth the grounds on which this authority rests, and gives an *ex cathedra* definition of agnosticism to the world at large. His prompt repudiation of Mr. Laing's pretensions may possibly have the salutary effect of quelling insubordination within the agnostic fold. But it is quite evident that there are ambitious pretenders and usurpers, and that the pontiff of agnosticism has need of a watchful eye if he wishes to preserve his prerogatives free from future encroachments. Mr. Laing seems to have been completely "scotched if not slain," for he does not appear anywhere to have come to the defence of his "eight articles," and as these articles have been already condemned by the head of his Church, we, too, may be pardoned if we imitate Professor Huxley in ignoring them, and turn to an examination of the accepted orthodox creed of agnosticism as established by its real founders.

The Agnosticism of Professor Huxley, however, or his claims, cannot be so easily set aside. He is the avowed champion of agnosticism, and claims large credit for its existence, and the only matter to be regretted is that his elucidation of it is not as clear as his championship is vigorous. He invests himself with complete and supreme authority. He relates the story of its origin, its baptism, and his sponsorship. He speaks as one having knowledge, and not as their scribes and pharisees, but, unfortunately, even in his hands agnosticism grows more and more nebulous, and his authoritative definition will be found quite as unsatisfactory in the realm of obligation as in the realm of faith. His definition of it is hopelessly inexact, and in its elasticity may mean very much or very little. "Agnosticism," he tells us in his condemnation of Mr. Laing, "is not a creed, but a method, the essence of which lies in the rigorous application of a single principle. . . Positively the principle may be expressed: In matters of intellect follow your reason as far as it will take

---

1 *Nineteenth Century*, February, 1889.

you without regard to any other
consideration; and negatively in
matters of the intellect, do not pre-
tend that conclusions are certain
which are not demonstrated or
demonstrable. That I take to be
the agnostic faith which, if a man
keep whole and undefiled, he shall
not be ashamed to look the universe
in the face whatever the future
may have in store for him." In explanation he adds: " The results of
the working out of the agnostic principle will vary according to individual knowledge and capacity, and
according to the general condition
of science. . . . . The only negative
fixed points will be those negations
which flow from the demonstrable
limitations of our faculties."

Taken in their broad sense, and
omitting his annexed explanation,
the positive and negative express-
ions of what he is pleased to denomi-
nate the agnostic principle are words
worthy either of agnostic or Christian, and it may be remarked in pass-

ing that if this be the agnostic faith, then are we all agnostics, (with, of course, a full acknowledgment of our infirmities and shortcomings after Mr. Huxley's own example), and that if he makes this the sole test of the agnostic faith pure and undefiled, he will find that he has a far larger following than he was aware of; and as this following will include the larger portion of believers in the inspired epistles and synoptic gospels, he may find it necessary to resort to wholesale excommunication and anathema. More recently he says:[1] "This principle may be stated in various ways, but they all amount to this: that it is wrong for a man to say that he is certain of the objective truth of any proposition unless he can produce evidence which logically justifies that certainty. This is what agnosticism asserts, and, in my opinion, it is all that is essential to agnosticism." We may pause a moment to inquire: Is Mr. Huxley's

---

[1] *Nineteenth Century*, June, 1889.

view of agnosticism broadening as
the years pass by? Or is it simply a
broadening of his acquaintance with
great principles? Establishing agnosticism on a principle held in common and practiced by all the world
is like establishing a sect on the
principle of gravitation or on the
proposition: all men must die. The
principle that it is wrong to believe
propositions as certain without satisfactory principle put on as possibly
evidence, quite
may be a perfect novelty to the "men
of science," as indeed the history
of speculative science would seem
to indicate; and if so, that they
should emphasize their joy upon its
discovery by forthwith establishing
a new *ism* to commemorate it with
this principle as its corner-stone is
certainly evidence of right-minded-
ness, but it is to be hoped that there
is no other portion of the intelligent
world on which the discovery is yet
to dawn. Surely this principle is
not a whit more agnostic than it is
Gnostic, or Christian, or Jewish, or

Turkish, or heathen. Enunciated in the form given by Professor Huxley, Jew and Gentile, Greek and barbarian, philosopher and Bushman can lay equal claim to it; but what is even more to the point, it is a very easy matter to show Professor Huxley that his agnosticism does not rest on this principle at all. Indeed, he himself seems to be perplexed about the basis of his agnosticism. The breadth and elasticity which he has recently been pleased to give it would indicate that he had misgivings, or that he was not quite sure of his bearings, or perhaps that he is meditating a change of front. It is quite possible that Professor Huxley is keenly sensitive to the ignominious position of his agnosticism, established, as it is, on a mere negation, and is trying to rescue it from its ignoble position and clothe it with a fictitious semblance of dignity by vainly imagining it to be established on a principle. But withal it rests on a mere negation.

The essence of agnosticism consists
in its denial of Christianity. The
agnosticism of our day is the only
agnosticism of which the world has
ever heard, and manifestly the agnosticism of our day simply consists,
in spite of Mr. Huxley's broad and
dazzling principles, in its rejection
of Christianity. Take away Christianity and the agnostic's occupation
is gone. Therefore it rests not on a
general principle, but on a mere negation. And should Professor Huxley
feel disposed to deny this, I can only
appeal from Philip drunk to Philip
sober, from Professor Huxley of the
"Nineteenth Century" articles to
Professor Huxley of former and better days. Time was when scientific
giants, intoxicated with the new
wine, strode with the strut of con-
scious science, and spoke in no fal-
tering voice. These were the days
when, if science was a coy, she was
also a dazzling mistress, and when,
in the full beam of her all too treach-
erous smile, Professor Huxley's tone
was confident and his rhetoric reson-

ant. It was in these halcyon days,
when victory seemed easy that he
wrote of agnosticism as[1] " that modern way of thinking which has been
called agnosticism from its profession of an incapacity to discover the
indisputable conditions of either
positive or negative knowledge in
many propositions, respecting which
not only the vulgar but philosophers
of the more sanguine sort revel in
the luxury of unqualified assurance."
Surely agnosticism here is founded,
not on a principle, but on an individual incapacity. It has the semblance of being based on the particular application of a principle, but
that particular application is neither
self-evident nor proven. And in the
hands of all agnostics, Mr. Spencer
excepted, all proof of this application is evaded by simply taking it
for granted.

It might, in passing, be pertinently
asked: Has Professor Huxley always
adhered to what he calls the agnostic principle ? What portion of the

[1] *Hume*, by Professor Huxley.

speculative science whicn Mr. Huxley has so dogmatically proclaimed
from the housetops will bear a "rigorous application" of this principle ?
Even in the days of evolutionary
wisdom was it always the golden rule
of the agnostic leader? But since
Professor Huxley himself has confessed that agnostics who never fail
in carrying out this principle are "as
rare as other people of whom the
same consistency can be truthfully
predicated," and in tones of deep
contrition adds,[1] " I am deeply con-
scious how far I myself fall short of
this ideal," it would be wanton
cruelty to make a digest of scientific
transgressions of the so-called agnostic principle. This wavering and un-
certainty, however, is evidence that
Professor Huxley has strong misgivings that everything is not right
with the agnostic position, and that
he does not feel exactly at ease regarding the stability of his once
vaunted fortress. In one place he

---

[1] *Nineteenth Century*, February 1889.

20

will tell us that "the only negative fixed points will be those negations which flow from the demonstrable limitations of our faculties." Again he will tell us of his "incapacity to discover the traces of either positive or negative knowledge," etc. And again he will tell us that he does[1] "not care very much to speak of anything as unknowable." Yet although his agnosticism is assuming vague and shadowy forms, nowhere does he attempt to apply it except against the truths of Christianity. And hence, since he has an agnosticism of theory and an agnosticism of practice, it is necessary to designate the latter by its proper title— anti-Christian agnosticism—to render it in some measure tangible, and bring it into harmony with the agnosticism of the day. Indeed, in spite of the broad sweep which Mr. Huxley is inclined to give to his agnostic method, it is no better or no worse than any individual agnosticism of the day, not even excepting

---
[1] *Nineteenth Century*, June, 1889.

Mr. Spencer's. There is, in all of them, a common subtratum, and on it all of the superstructures are raised. The essence of all agnosticism consists in one common agnostic superstition, and to it all of them are reducible, viz., that Christianity is a deadly enemy to all falsehood, to false philosophy, as well as to false science. It has therefore been decided by common consent that the truths of Christianity are not the proper objects of knowledge; that if a thing cannot be adequately known because it is beyond the reach of our faculties, that neither should it be believed, and that no amount of testimony should justify us in admitting it to a hearing. A further rule of action would seem to be that if a thing be not wholly within reach of our faculties, nothing will justify us in believing it, but, on the contrary, it is our duty to ignore and deny it, and treat it as pure fiction ; and that consequently anti-Christian agnosticism is justified and sanctified in opposing Christianity, and is all the more deserving of merit if at all times and in all places it wages a ceaseless warfare against it.

It matters little whether Mr. Huxley rejects the unknowable in name if he retains it in reality. And that he retains it in principle is patent on the face of his papers. And this brings us to

The Agnosticism of Mr. Spencer and the Unknowable.

For Mr. Spencer, in spite of all Mr. Huxley's pretensions, is really the author of agnosticism. Mr. Huxley may have introduced the name, but Mr. Spencer created the thing. Agnosticism is the natural outgrowth of the unknowable. The unknowable is not only the god of agnosticism, but it is its creator as well. The philosophy of either is the philosophy of both, and Mr. Spencer alone has undertaken to give us a philosophy of either. Mr. Spencer enunciates the definition of agnosticism in clearer and more precise terms than Mr. Huxley. He says,[1] "The name agnosticism fitly expresses the confessed inability to know or conceive the nature of the power manifested through pheno- mena." Here, at least, we have something clear—the definite if de- fective meaning and purpose of ag- nosticism. It is the inability, and inability not only to know but also the inability to conceive something very definite, viz., the nature of the power manifested through pheno- mena. This narrows down agnos- ticism to its proper limits, and saves the trouble of making distinctions between a vague and indefinite ag- nosticism which embraces all lovers of truth and that which we have been forced, in Professor Huxley's case, for the sake of clearness, to desig- nate anti-Christian agnosticism. It is not, of course, satisfactory as a definition, but it is vastly preferable to Mr. Huxley's generalities, inas- much as it circumscribes the domain of agnosticism. In Mr. Spencer's

[1] *The Nature and Reality of Religion—Retrogress- ive Religion.*

hands, too, agnosticism takes a more
exacting and imperative form.
" Duty," he tells us," requires us to
submit ourselves with all humility
to the established limits of our intelligence," and therefore under the
stern pressure of duty he undertook
to construct for us the agnostic
philosophy of the unknowable. Mr.
Spencer has given us two distinct
allocutions on this subject; one in
his " First Principles," the other in
his controversy with Mr. Harrison.

His Reverential Motive.

Mr. Spencer found man on far
too intimate relations with his
Creator. His heart was sorely
grieved and his spirit groaned within him on beholding the sacrilegious
familiarity with which men wor-
shipped their Deity. It was an in-
dignity offered to the Infinite Uncaused that man should presume to
know anything whatsoever upon the
subject, or that the Infinite Energy
should be considered capable of

stooping to solve for man the mysteries which so perplex him. The pious revelled in impiety, and religion luxuriated in irreligion to a degree that aroused all the righteous indignation of Mr. Spencer's reverent nature. It must not, it shall not be. The Infinite Uncaused, was not shrouded in mystery dark and deep enough. The pillars of heaven were too low, the clouds that veiled the Infinite were not sufficiently dense. The curtained folds of mystery were not dark enough. The pillars of heaven must be heightened. The Absolute must be thrown further back into the deep azure. The Self-existent must be enthroned on the darkest clouds whose mystery shall be impenetrable. Deep must be added unto deep, and abyss linked to abyss to place between the Infinite and the daring impiety of man

---

1 First Principles : § 28. " Religion has ever been more or less irreligious, and it continues to be partially irreligious even now." And elsewhere he characterizes the profession of a knowledge of the relation of the creature to the Creator as "transcendent audacity."

an endless chaos, the greatness of
which shall awe and humble into
quietude the restless mind of man.
The darkest clouds of deepest mid-
night must be interwoven, and fold
upon fold of mystery added until a
curtain is drawn between man's reason and the Absolute so mysterious
and awe-inspiring that even omnipotence cannot pierce it, and omni-
presence be powerless to penetrate
it. Not only the profaneness of in-
solent inquiry and prying curiosity
must be shut out, but even the worship that bends in lowliest homage before the Sovereign dominion
must be told it is sacrilege, and the
prayerful words that would bless
and praise the sovereign majesty
must be accounted either meaning-
less mummery or highest blasphemy.
The solemnity of the deep and aw-
ful silence no man must dare to
break. Not even to omnipotence
itself will this privilege be accorded.
And this Mr. Spencer has assured us
is not atheism, it is science. It is

" our highest wisdom and our highest duty." *Inconceivable* and *incomprehensible* were terms with which religious minds were long familiar.
But they were not acceptable to the
soul of Mr. Spencer. They were
not sufficiently water-tight, or air-
tight, or thought-tight to exclude an
omni~~potent~~ *present* deity from the mind of
man. Mr. Spencer's mission was to
rid the world of the incubus of a personal God, and these terms—do what
he would—would not exclude Him
from thought. The world was filled
with this idea, and the conception
must be effectually driven out and
kept out. Hence he was forced to
cast about for a new term which
would fill every nook and cranny
and crevice of thought, and effectually bar from thought that which
strangely enough he tells us is present in every thought. And so he in-
vented the philosophy of the *Unknowable* of his " First Principles."
And let us not mistake his purpose.
In his controversy with Mr. Harrison he has delineated the Unknow-

able in more vivid coloring. Whatever men might have justly surmised heretofore matters not. Now there is no chance of misconception. It was not that religion might be wholly abolished that Mr. Spencer created the Unknowable. It was that Mr. Spencer should have the supreme satisfaction of introducing his own religion and creating his own deity. He has taken away our God, and we know not where he has laid Him, but he does not mean to leave us without an object of worship. He takes the Unknowable from its obscurity. He makes a full profession of faith in it. He holds it up for our inspection. In his second sketch he draws the outlines more clearly, the features are more fully developed, the proportions are on a larger scale. He partially unveils it. It is a little less vague and dim than when we first saw it. It is, however, the agnostic idol, actually set up for homage and adoration. It is the duly authorized ob-

ject of worship. It is the venerable,
the adorable, the lovable Unknowable. Down, agnostics, on your
knees! Let us worship and adore!

Mr. Spencer's Object.

It was the laudable ambition of
Mr. Spencer to effectually put
Christianity out of court altogether.
But how was he to accomplish it? He
could not disprove it. He could not
dislodge it. Could he not persuade
the world to ignore it? The conception was an inspiration! and he in-
dustriously set to work to construct a
philosophy which would serve the
lofty purpose. He made the discovery that the position of the human mind towards the truths of
Christianity was unique and wholly
without parallel; that man's mind
was related to religious truth as it
was to no other subject, that the
"unseen world" could not be known
in exactly the same manner as we
know the world of sense. Men
could not see the God whom they

worshiped, the heaven of their hopes, or the hell of their fears, as they could gaze upon mountain, rock or river. The objects of men's beliefs were not palpable entities like the falling rain or the growing corn. They could not be measured by a carpenter's rule, or weighed in the chemist's balance. Our knowledge of the truths of Christianity was wholly unlike our knowledge of the world in which we live. However cogent the claims or strong the testimony in their favor, there was always a chance for cavil as to the terms and extent of our knowledge of them. Nay, was it not the boast of Christianity that its kingdom was not of this world, that it was of a supernatural order? Manifestly, then, the best way was to treat it as non-existent, to utterly ignore it. This was the proper attitude of men towards it. Might it not be just as well, too, at once, to cease mincing matters and clear the distance at a single bound? Had we really any knowledge about such things, any information that could be called cognition? Was Christianity really demonstrable to the human intellect? Of a surety it did not conform to the rules and standards by which we decide that we really do know what comes within reach of our faculties. Decidedly, then, it were sheer folly to waste time upon it. Let man be reasonable, let him close his doors resolutely against it, absolutely deny it a hearing, and pronounce it at once and forever—*Unknowable.* This was not only wisdom but duty. All pretended information on the subject was unintelligible. Christianity did not admit of demonstration. Where there was no knowledge, not even conception, there was no room for credibility, Hence it was a species of *de non apparentibus et non existentibus eadem est ratio.* If the judicial process was short and summary, it was but a slight wrenching of the laws of evidence to treat such truths as non-existent; nay, to make it a duty so to treat them. Hume had already perceived all this and counselled this method. Mr. Spencer perceived it, and set to work with a right hearty good will to base upon it his philosophy of *the Unknowable.* But above and before all, Mr. Spencer must preserve at least a semblance of judicial justice. He must be no more partial to science than to religion. And he sat him down in the seat of judgment to calmly weigh the merits of *ultimate* religious *ideas,* and *ultimate scientific ideas.* But the judge's balance suddenly becomes a magician's wand, and under the magic touch of Mr. Spencer's philosophy, ultimate religious ideas ; the infinite, the absolute, the unconditioned; and ultimate scientific ideas ; space, time, force, etc., and all else which like these transcend experience, drift away dim shadows into agnostic dreamland, vanish wholly from sight for a moment only to blend somewhere in that unknown realm and emerge again into full view, to be forever after one and inseparable; henceforward to be known as the unknowable. Henceforth there exist but the knowable and the Unknowable. Through all future time the Unknowable is God, agnosticism is its religion, and Herbert Spencer is its prophet.

Here, then, was the long-sought answer to Christianity. At last this pushing, obtrusive Christianity was got rid of, by ruling it out of court decisively. Here was its answer which should silence it forever. It was unintelligible. It was unthinkable. It was unknowable. If things are unknowable, of course they cannot be known. If they are unintelligible surely they cannot be understood. What we cannot know— why, of course, we cannot know, "and there's an end on't." The unknowable is unknowable to the end of reckoning, and what use of further inquiry. From its very appellation the unknowable remains unknown, and is at once dropped out of sight to sink into oblivion, as the plummet sinks to the bottom of the wave.

In the agnostic method there was, moreover, this tremendous advantage. Nothing was hazarded. No proposition was advanced, and consequently refutation need not be dreaded. Negations are usually safe and impregnable. The smallest possible front was presented to the enemy, and shot and shell could be safely showered in torrents from this vantage ground without fear of a return fire.

Such a position, it is true, does not indicate a very high degree of courage, and would seem to justify the rather graceless *soubriquet* of " cowardly agnosticism" which has been lately bestowed upon it. But this unassailable position was regarded as its strength. It seemed to be fashioned after the style of the new ships of war which are supposed to rise above the water for a moment for their deadly fire and instantly disappear again beneath the waves. Con-

sequently it was regarded as a mas-
terpiece of military tactics, of dia-
lectical engineering, but it is simply,
as I hope to show, a masterstroke of
ingenious folly. Such was the
structure of marvellous architectural
ingenuity which Mr. Spencer devised
and planned, and then at once set to
work to establish on a solid and per-
manent foundation. It was essential
that it should be deeply and strongly based, and accordingly he laid
down *the laws of knowledge* in his
philosophy of the Unknowable and
framed them with a view to filling
all requirements.

Mr. Spencer's Philosophy.

In his efforts to construct a philosophy of agnosticism, Mr. Spencer
took a careful survey of the way in
which knowledge is attained. He
made a careful analysis of our ultimate religious ideas and our ultimate scientific ideas. He pondered
deeply the relativity of all knowledge. He decided that to be known,
a thing must be known as a relation,

as a difference, or as a likeness, otherwise it cannot be classed, and therefore cannot be known. "Whatever does not present each of these does not admit of cognition." He tried the Infinite, the Absolute, the Power behind all phenomena by these standards of knowledge. He concluded it could not be known as a relation, it could not be known as a difference, it could not be known as a likeness. The unconditioned presented none of these elements of cognition, hence it is trebly unthinkable. He went further still, and defined the limitations of thought. He called in Sir William Hamilton and Dean Mansel to aid him. He found that the Infinite, the Absolute stretched away immeasurably beyond the limits of our faculties, and hence was absolutely inconceivable. He was not, however, content to rest satisfied with this, but above and before all he lays down new standards of his own by which to test our cognitions. He establishes and defines his *symbolic con-*

ceptions of the legitimate and illegitimate order. In this consists the essence of his entire philosophy of the Unknowable. It is the mainspring of his entire line of thought. It is the pivot on which turn his views of cognition. It is the sum and substance of his philosophy, and the basis of all agnosticism. I give the entire passage in full. The italics are mine.

1 " To sum up, we must say of conceptions in general, that they are complete only when the attributes of the object conceived are of such a number and kind that they can be represented in consciousness so nearly at the same time as to seem all present together; that as the objects conceived become larger and more complex, some of the attributes first thought of fade from consciousness before the rest have been represented, and the conception thus becomes imperfect; that when the size, complexity, or discreteness of the object conceived becomes very great, only a small portion of its attributes can be thought of at once, and the conception formed of it thus becomes so inadequate as to form a mere symbol; that nevertheless such symbolic conceptions which are indispensable in general thinking are *legitimate provided* that by some cumulative or indirect process of thought, or by the fulfillment of predictions based on them, we can assure ourselves that they stand

---

1 *First Principles*, § 9.

for actualities; but when our symbolic conceptions are such that *no cumulative or indirect process of thought* can enable us to *ascertain that there are no corresponding actualities, nor any predictions be made whose fulfillment can prove this, then* they are altogether *vicious and illusive*, and in no way distinguishable *from pure fictions*."

He adds:

" And now to consider the bearings of this general truth (?) on our immediate topic—Ultimate Religious Ideas."

It is very evident, then, that he stakes everything on the working of this grand " general truth," and that it was formulated with the especial view of covering the entire ground occupied by religious ideas. Surely here is enough to silence all theologians. All their talk is, as Professor Huxley would call it, "senseless babble." It is "illegitimate." All conceptions of God "are illusive and in no way distinguishable from pure fictions." Conceivability is the only ground of certitude. Credibility is wholly excluded.

In this short synopsis I have, I think, given the essence of the agnostic philosophy. I think Mr. Spencer himself would be willing to admit that I have given the cardinal and vital points of his chapters on the Unknowable. And now, with God's blessing, I shall, in simple fashion, proceed to do it full and signal justice.

Refutation of Agnosticism.

There are many ways of refuting the philosophy of the Unknowable. It could be easily be shown that Mr. Spencer, in working it out, has fallen into more than one intellectual suicide. It could be proved that it is utterly useless for the purpose of excluding revelation. It could be proved that, followed to its legitimate consequences metaphysically, it leads directly to complete nescience. But all these methods would involve metaphysical reasoning, which the majority of agnostics might find to be dry and difficult to follow. Hence, as it is sometimes found that the best way to get rid of an absurd law is to enforce it, I believe that the best way to show the absurdity of the agnostic philosophy is to insist upon a "rigorous application" of it wherever the method is applicable.

Is it then the duty of the human mind to ignore everything it cannot grasp? Is it, as Hume has told us, our duty to make war upon beliefs and "subjects utterly inaccessible to our understanding?" Is it the highest wisdom and highest duty of men " to declare unknowable and treat as non-existent whatever is beyond the reach of their faculties? Let us see: A slight examination is sufficient to discover that there are many instances where *cognition of appearances* is as absolutely impossible as *cognition of the reality which transcends all appearances*. It is a well-known axiom in philosophy, attributed, I believe, to Aristotle, that nothing can be in the mind but what is first in the senses. *Nihil est in intellectu, quod prius non fuerit in sensu.* Consequently, it is obvious that men cannot form any conceptions properly so-called of things unless they possess the faculties by which such conceptions are formed. A man born blind can form no conception of the light of day. A man born without the sense of hearing cannot be made made to understand what we mean by the note of the nightingale or the peal of the thunder. In vain do we undertake to explain the meaning of the scent of the rose or the violet to him who has never been gifted with the sense of smell. Every one has heard of the blind man, who, when asked what conception he formed of purple, said that he thought it must resemble the sound of a trumpet. Such are our conceptions of the known world when the faculty by which we form these conceptions is wanting. It is a melancholy fact, only too common, that many men are born into the world without the use of one or more of their senses, and that consequently the knowledge or cognitions in the acquisition of which the absent sense is a necessary medium, they can never attain. Such knowledge is beyond the reach of their faculties. The notions of such things are to them utterly inconceivable. Here is an instructive parallel, and it will be interesting to pursue it further. Be it observed that the only reason why men are agnostics is because they cannot conceive or know the power which lies behind phenomena. Professor Huxley will tell us with lachrymose air that such things are beyond the reach of his " poor faculties," and Mr. Spencer will tell us that our conceptions of such things are " of the illegitimate order and in no way distinguishable from pure fictions." Take, for instance, the case of a man born blind. The relation of the agnostic mind to the truths of Christianity is precisely the relation[1] of a man born blind to the light of day, as far as knowledge or conception goes. The idea of light is wholly beyond his powers of conception ; as Professor Huxley would

[1] My meaning, of course, is that there is an absolute impossibility of conception in either case.

put it, is entirely out of the reach of his faculties. Without the sense of sight his mind is no more capable of conceiving an adequate idea, or indeed any idea at all of light or its nature than the agnostic says he is of conceiving an adequate idea of the Absolute, or the Infinite Uncaused, or of Mr. Spencer's Unknowable. The faculty by which he might form the conception—the sense of sight—is absent, just as the faculty of conceiving the Infinite is wanting to the agnostic. Sight for the blind man transcends all experience.

As far as he is concerned, and the entire class to which he belongs, the nature or existence of light is neither "demonstrated or demonstrable." He can confess, over and over again, in the language of Mr. Spencer, "his inability to know or conceive the nature" of light, just as strongly as he bewails his "inability to know or to conceive the nature of the power manifested through phenomena." Both are to him a closed book, a fountain sealed up. The idea of light is to him "rigorously inconceivable." The axiom *nihil intellectu, quod non fuerit prius in sensu,* exercises a logical tyranny, and he cannot escape its despotism. Sight is for him literally unthinkable, even more so than the Unknowable, for here there is no element that transcends consciousness to force the fact of its existence into every thought. Does duty then require him "to submit himself with all humility to the established limits of his intelligence?" May he not listen with attention to a lover of nature who speaks of the glow of sunset, the pearly dew drop in the sunset, the beauty of the landscape, or the tints of the rainbow? Will Mr. Spencer scoff and Professor Huxley sneer if he should happen to speak of white or blue, the verdure of the mossy bank, or the azure of the heavens? Even when he longs for the gift of vision to look upon the passing clouds or the hues of flowers, must he do so in

secret, lest some agnostic make
merry over his folly, and cover him
with ridicule because he hopes for
things of whose existence he can
know nothing? Will Mr. Spencer
permit him to entertain, even on the
authority of Professor Tyndall, the
foolish notion that there is light
which possibly he may one day see?
Must he be absolutely and eternally
silent upon this subject? Must
" the negative fixed points" for him
"be those negations which flow from
the demonstrable limitation of his
faculties" The "demonstrable limitation of his faculties," will certainly not include the ability to
conceive light or color, and when
agnostics undertake to restrict
him to these limits, is he to
follow the example of Professor
Huxley by practicing the apostolic
injunction to " suffer fools gladly,"
or must he place no reliance whatever on the testimony of men? Is it
his duty to proclaim himself a blind
agnostic, and light as unknowable?
Must he ever incontinently bewail his

manifest "incapacity," and tell men
who would persuade him of the existence of light and color, and explain their nature, that "they revel
in the luxury of unqualified assurance." He can no more conceive
the idea of light than[1] "the idea of a
square fluid or a moral substance."
Must he, consequently, with petulant
tone, tell the advocates of the foolish
theory of light, that "it is not a
question of probability or credibility, but of conceivability." Or will
any amount of testimony bear down
the agnostic principle? And if so,
what amount of testimony? And if
it can be overthrown by the testimony of men, so that we may, in de-
fiance of it, believe their testimony,
what, then, becomes of the principle?
By "no cumulative or indirect processes of thought" can the blind "ascertain that there are corresponding actualities" to his symbolic conceptions of light, nor can any pre-
diction of his be made whose fulfil-

[1] *First Principles.*

ment can prove that such exist, must he therefore conclude that they are "altogether vicious and illusive, and in no way distinguishable from pure fictions," and treat them as non-existent. Must he submit to Mr. Spencer's symbols of the illegitimate order, and conclude that light is to him in his present condition literally unthinkable, rigorously inconceivable, absolutely unknowable? Must he scoff at all such folly, and scorn all vain inquiry?

By pursuing the matter further, it will be found, that if agnosticism possesses any validity at all against Christianity, it possesses not only an equal, but a stronger validity in this case. It becomes an *a fortiori* in the case of the blind against the existence of light. The only consideration which Mr. Spencer found to justify him in retaining the God of religion, even under the ignominious guise of the Unknowable, was that he found it an element of every state of consciousness; an element, too,[1] "which persists at all times, under all circumstances, and cannot cease until consciousness ceases," an indestructible element of thought, and one to get rid of the consciousness of which is an absolute impossibility. But no such consideration will justify the agnostic blind man in retaining the light of day even as a possible existence. If, as he tells us, "*the only possible measure of relative validity* among our beliefs is the degree of their persistence in opposition to the efforts made to change them," and if it follows that this "which persists at all times, under all circumstances, and cannot cease until consciousness ceases, has the highest validity of any;" does it not follow inversely that the belief which has no persistence has no validity, and that consequently the blind man's belief in a world of sight and light has for him no existence for it has no persistence.

Again, let us suppose that our blind man is an agnostic follower of

---

[1] *First Principles.*

Mr. Spencer. Side by side, then, with his ignorance about God and the Unknowable, is his ignorance of the *visible* world. Everything that he as an agnostic can predicate about the former he can predicate with equal truth about the latter. He cannot conceive the light of day as absolute; he cannot conceive it as relative. He cannot conceive it as limited ; he cannot conceive it as unlimited. He cannot conceive it as conditioned ; he cannot conceive it as unconditioned. "Thought," Mr. Spencer tells us, "involves relation, difference, likeness; whatever does not present each of these three does not admit of cognition." But he cannot think of light as a relation; he cannot think of it as a difference; he cannot think of it as a likeness; he cannot think of it as all three, for the simple reason that he cannot think of it at all. He can form no conception of it, whether in itself, or in relation or comparison with anything known to him; and must he

hence conclude that like the Unconditioned, it is trebly unthinkable?
But while the Unconditioned possesses for him that indestructible
element of consciousness which he
can by no means rid himself of; and
which justifies him in pronouncing
the Unknowable to at least exist,
nay, compels him to admit it; on the
other hand, in his search after
knowledge of light, he finds this element of persistence strikingly absent, and nothing to justify him, in
the face of all his *a priori* reasoning, in admitting its existence. So
that he finds that every objection
which, as an agnostic, he can bring
against the truths of Christianity or
the unseen world, he can bring not
only with equal but with far greater
force against the seen world. This
is a reasoning from which there is
no possible escape for the agnostic.
The blind man cannot examine light
from the standpoint of our knowledge of light. We must examine it
from the standpoint of his ignorance,

and put ourselves in his place. And if the agnostic position toward Christianity is the correct one, it follows that the same attitude is the correct one for a man born blind to assume towards the world of light.

Further, let us assume the case of an asylum for the blind where there might happen to be a considerable number who were born without the sense of sight. And let us further suppose that amongst the latter there were two or three bold, independent spirits, athirst for knowledge, impatient of old methods, with a love of philosophical research like Mr. Spencer, with the pugnacious propensities of Mr. Huxley, daring, enterprising champions of intellectual freedom, haters of the old, lovers of the new, with a laudable ambition to aid and enlighten their fellows, to strike the shackles from human thought, and emancipate if not the entire human family, at least that microcosm in which they lived, from the thraldom of ancient superstitions. Having mastered well their

Kant and their Hume, and their
Spencer, and with the spirit of a
Huxley *plus* a little seasoning of
sound logic, going forth conquering
and to conquer, they have become
thoroughly imbued with agnosticism and unknowabilism, and at last
they turn their attention to the question of sight and light. Here, too,
was a question on which the world
lorded it over them with an affecta·
tion of superior wisdom and knowledge, just as in matters of religion.
Did not men insult their intelligence
by pitying their blindness, and
speaking sympathizingly of their
darkness ? What in reality was this
sight and light of which men spoke
with " the luxury of unqualified assurance ?" What was this shade,
this color, which even "the man of
science" spoke gibly of ? Assuredly
here was another superstition which
agnosticism had overlooked and
which it was their bounden duty to
overthrow. Why not rise in rebellion against it at once ? Why not

betake themselves at once to the heights of their agnostic superiority and look down with supreme scorn on those who maintained that there existed an " unseen world" of light and color? Surely all conception of it was just as impossible as the conception of the infinite, the absolute, nay more so, for in the latter case there was an ever-present consciousness which would not away, while in the former there was but a huge blank, utter vacuity. Why not, as true agnostic disciples of Mr. Spencer, rule such notions out of court altogether? Were they not unthinkable, inconceivable, unknowable ? Was it not their " highest wisdom as well as well as their highest duty" to regard them as such ? Why not at once enlist all their blind brethren in open rebellion against this vaunted superiority not only of knowledge, but even of powers? And at once they begin to preach their agnostic gospel of demolition of this idol. To them comes Mr. Spencer with " Hold, my good friends; you are wrong and rash. Let me read to you, my friend, Mr. Proctor, on the beauty of the starry heavens; let me introduce to you, my friend, Mr. Tyndall, who will explain to you the nature and properties of light. Be not rash, be not hasty. All the world will hold you in derision; be persuaded by me. Even the undulating theory of light is very beautiful when you come to understand it."

" But," reply our blind agnostics, " we have studied this question of sight carefully again and again in the light of your teachings, and we are forced to the conclusion that it is ' beyond the reach of our faculties.' Have you yourself not taught us with Hume, nay insisted, that " duty requires us to submit ourselves with all humility to the established limits of our intelligence"? Even Professor Huxley, whom we revere even as yourself, has but the other day taught us that ' it is immoral to say that there are propositions which men ought to believe; without logically satisfactory evidence,' and this in this case we cannot possibly have. All our conceptions of light are as you have taught us, oh wise and good master! merely symbolic conceptions of the legitimate order, and 'no cumulative or indirect processes can enable us to ascertain that there are corresponding actualties,' nor can any predictions be made whose fulfillment can prove this to us; are we not therefore to regard them as 'altogether vicious and illusive, and in no way distinguishable from pure fictions?'"

"But," says Mr. Spencer, "you must believe me. Just as you can hear with your ears, or feel with your hands, so you could see light with your eyes had you the faculty of vision. Trust me, there is a world of sight of which you know nothing." To which we get the answer, "O trusted and learned teacher, long since have we learned of you the true principles of knowledge. You ask us to *believe* you, and it is probable you may be right, Yet of this we have our own opinion ; but 'it is not a question of probability and credibility, but of conceivability,' as one of your own wise maxims hath it. Or, again, we cannot 'put together in consciousness' the notions upon which you insist, Heat we know and cold we know ; but this light, what is it ? as your great colleague Mr. Huxley would put it. But to us this notion of light is according to your own expression 'rigorously inconceivable.' How, then, can you consistenly ask us to believe it ?"

Mr. Spencer, of course, is naturally perplexed at this unlooked for but at the same time just application of his method, and feels the full force of the logic of their position, and at last in despair looses his hold upon his principles and turns for refuge to credibility, and with a full sense that even if in opposition to his own philosophy, he is at last on solid ground, says " but all mankind believes in the existence of sight and light, nay they know the world of sight. Hear the voice of all the world and believe." But it is with reproach they now turn from him and say, " False, lost leader ! Hast thou brought us into the wilderness there to desert us ? False-hearted ! dost thou play false to thy own principles. Thou has taught us to put conceivability far above credibility, and now when it pleaseth thee dost thou reverse the order ? Thou has laid down rules and established principles, and thou hast not the courage to consistently pursue them to their logical conclusions. If conceivability, then, is to yield to credibility contrary to thy former wise maxims, at what point must it yield ? To what amount of testimony ? Has thou found that a certain amount of testimony will form a counterpoise for the absence or impossibility of conception ? If, so then at what point will the scale be turned in favor of testimony ? But even if thou shouldst thus play false to thy own maxims, and decide in

favor of testimony by saying that
we must yield to the opinions of the
rest of mankind, know that thou dost
tear down the barriers which thou
hast opposed to the Unknowable.
And know, too, that we have but too
faithfully studied thy lessons, and
have learned from thee also the con-
clusive answer which is shown 'by a
survey of the past, that majorities
have usually been wrong.' And is
it not likely that, as usual, it is true
in this case? Avaunt! thou traitor
to thy own teachings! Thou has
builded better than thou didst
know. Thou has uttered truths and
been a deserter from them, but it
will go hard with us or we shall
better thy teachings, and we pledge
ourselves to preach the true and
comprehensive gospel of agnosticism as well against the *seen* world
as against 'the unseen world,' in
season and out of season. And since
thou art false, then shall we take to
ourselves for a leader instead of thee
thine own condisciple of nobler

mettle and daring, and who feareth
not consistency nor inconsistency—
Professor Huxley himself. In his
very latest instruction on this subject hath he given us full warrant
to carry our agnosticism to any
pitch we choose, for with his broad
views unhesitatingly expressed, he
says : ' The extent of the region of
the uncertain, the number of the
problems the investigation of which
ends in a verdict of not proven will
vary according to the knowledge
and the intellectual habits of the individual agnostic.' And surely the
verdict in this case for us will be ' not
proven.' And in his great scientific
wisdom he hath this further :
'What I am sure about is that there
are many topics about which I know
nothing ; and which, so far as I can
see, are out of the reach of my
faculties. But whether these things
are knowable by any one else is exactly one of those matters which is
beyond my knowledge, *though I may
have a tolerably strong opinion as to the
probabilities of the case.*' In these

wise words, even with the fore-knowledge of a prophet, doth he decide our case for us as if he were one of us. What you are pleased to call the world of sight is for us ' out of the reach of our faculties.' But to apply Professor Huxley's sage method of reasoning the matter ; whether this world of sight is knowable by you or by any one else is exactly one of those matters which is beyond our knowledge, though, pardon us, we have tolerably strong opinions as to whether you do know them. Indeed, to be candid, to us it appears as if you are the victims of a delusion. Furthermore, we shall follow the advice of Hume, the great protagonist of agnosticism, who tells us to wage a ceaseless warfare on subjects utterly inaccessible to our understanding, and since this world of sight is one of those subjects which ' human vanity' would fain investigate, it will receive from us no quarter."

What reply will Mr. Spencer make to this logical driving home of his

own philosophy? Nay, will not
Professor Huxley be inclined to
stare at this unlooked for application
of his pet method? But it will be
difficult for either the one or the
other to show reason why their
philosophy and its methods have
been applied illogically. If Mr.
Spencer and Mr. Huxley are right,
then are the blind right also. If
Mr. Spencer's argument is sound and
valid for the removal of God out of
court, then is their argument sound.
If the philosophy which culminates
in the Unknowable and treats it as
non-existent is right, then is the
man born blind justified in treating
with contempt all that the most
learned physicist can tell him about
the properties of light. The same
applies with equal force to that vast
multitude who fill our asylums for
deaf-mutes, and who have never
heard the music of a human voice.
The sun shines, is a proposition as
incomprehensible to a man born
blind as the proposition ; God
created the world, is to the most

sanguine of agnostic philosophers. The birds sing, would be a proposition quite as inconceivable to a man born deaf as the idea of three persons in one God is to a follower of Mr. Spencer. The ideas suggested by the first proposition is as intelligible to the one and to the other as the idea of square fluids or moral substances.

The incongruity of the agnostic position will be all the more striking if we reflect that there would be no more amusing scene than to see two or three blind men excitedly endeavoring to rouse a community by eloquence, by gesture, by impassioned argument, by appeal to reason and logic against the acceptation of the doctrines of a seen world, and turning the shafts of scorn and ridicule against those who clung to the ancient superstition. It certainly would be a spectacle for gods and men, and would be likely, too, to convulse both gods and men with laughter. But the real absurdity, more ridiculous than all, will appear when we reflect that their ludicrous behavior would be fully justified by the philosophy of agnosticism. If agnosticism be the golden rule of mankind—our highest duty and our highest wisdom alike—it will be found to produce strange conclusions even in the "knowable world." Is it not a most salutary reflection, then, and one which should restrain sanguine philosophers from a too ready dogmatism, that there exist commonplaces of our every-day life which men know to be among the most obvious realities of existence, but of which even the most remotely symbolic conceptions, are, to a certain portion of mankind, utterly inconceivable? If we close our eyes for a few moments and compare the darkness with the world of beauty which surrounds us and which becomes a reality to our senses when we again open our eyes, we may form a faint notion of the extent of their deprivation. This world of beauty is ever present to them just as it is to us. The sun in the heavens, the landscape with its varied tints, the sheen of verdure, all are at their doors, as close at hand to them as to us who know them, and yet are to them wholly unknown and unknowable. The intellectual faculties of those afflicted with this deprivation may be quite as keen, or even more so, than ours. Yet to them these facts are incomprehensible mysteries of the "knowable" world. In no possible way can we make to dawn on their minds the faintest conception of light. And yet a flood of golden light daily envelops them. Varied hues and brilliant coloring are as near to them as to other men; on all sides are they bathed in the sun's rays. The many-tinted flowers and the ever-changing clouds above their heads are as actual facts as the food they eat or the clothes they wear, and yet all these things are to their intellects utterly unfathomable.

And the seeming simplicity of the obstacle hindering these conceptions is equally surprising. Remove a little film, slightly change the conformation of the eye, let the retina undergo the slightest possible transformation, and a flood of radiant splendor bursts upon the vision, the inconceivable is conceived, the incomprehensible is fully comprehended, the unknowable is adequately known, our agnostics become gnostic—gods, knowing even as ourselves. That which could in no wise be presented in thought becomes as our most familiar thoughts.

And just as in this world of sense, this " knowable " world, there are objects of knowledge known to us, but wholly inconceivable by others who do not possess the faculty by which this knowledge is acquired ; in the same way St. Paul tells us there is an unseen world which we cannot know, [1] *"Quae sunt Dei, nemo novit nisi Spiritus Dei,"* but must

---

[1] The things also that are of God no man knoweth but the Spirit of God.

accept the testimony of beings who do. [1]"*Nobis autem revelavit Deus per spiritum suum*"; or as we find it in Ecclesiasticus, [2]"*Plurima supra sensum hominis ostensa sunt tibi.*" The question is not whether these things can be realized in thought, or whether we can comprehend them. The question is : Do they exist ? Will the film ever be removed from our eyes ? How can we live so that we may some day behold them in all the splendor of their undreamed reality? They may be as near to us as light is to the blind, and the question for us should be : When shall our senses be purified and our visions clarified, so that the visions of Peter, James and John on the Mount of Thabor, or that of the transported St. Paul may dawn upon our view, and fill us with a joy far surpassing that of him to whom it might be given after years of darkness for the first time to behold the visions of our own

---

[1] But to us God hath revealed them by his spirit.

[2] For many things are shown to thee above the understanding of men.

fair world. "The nature of the power behind phenomena" we certainly cannot know, because our faculties are not infinite. An adequate conception of God no sane man contends that he can have. That our intellects are finite is sufficient reason as well as sufficient proof that we cannot grasp the Infinite, but it is no reason, or furnishes no proof, that we cannot know something about God. The terms of the proposition which conveys the knowledge may not always be conceivable. We may not always be able to realize in thought both the subject and predicate, just as Mr. Spencer cannot realize in thought the Infinite or the Absolute which logic has forced upon him, or just as the proposition, the moon shines brightly, is incomprehensible to him who has never seen the light. But that is no reason why we should not assent to the proposition, properly accredited, in the hope that we may one day see more clearly and know more adequately. To rebel against the toleration of such propositions would be, as St. Thomas Aquinas tells us, to imitate the ignoramus (*idiotæ*), who would turn away from the propositions of Aristotle and pronounce them false because they were above his comprehension. It matters little whether we comprehend them now, or whether the confused, indefinite, inadequate conceptions are but the veriest shadows and symbols of the Infinite. We well know that the "veil" is yet before our eyes, that only "*ex parte cognoscimus*," that "we see through a glass darkly," and that the mystery cannot be solved on this side of the "veil." But if we are blear-eyed and blink blindly, as the owl and the bat at noonday, should we not be thankful for this instead of wilfully closing our eyes and shutting out the little light we do possess, especially if by using that little, we may hope some day to gaze without flinching, as boldly as the eagle at the noonday sun? Is it not the height of folly to despise the little we know because we do not know all ? As Locke tells us : " The candle that is set up in us shines bright enough for all purposes." As he well says, "our business here is not to know all things, but things which concern our conduct. It will be no excuse for an idle and untoward servant who would not attend to his business by candle-light, to plead that he had not broad sunshine." And most men will agree with him that " it is folly for men to quarrel with their own constitutions, and throw away the blessings their hands are filled with, because they are not big enough to grasp everything."

And yet this seems to be the agnostic method. And in this shallow, superficial age agnosticism is accepted—probably for its novelty. Mr. Spencer is hailed as a Daniel come to judgment when he proposes the exclusion of Christianity on the grounds of its unknowability. Agnosticism gets to be the fashion.

498408

And Mr. Spencer's philosophy has, it would appear, been introduced in some of our leading universities. If such be the seed, what nature of crop must we expect? Agnostic philosophy has been regarded by a few as the acme of intellectual greatness, I think I have shown that it is the nadir of intellectual imbecility. Let me conclude with this suggestion: If the sun, which with its train of light and glory gilds the hilltops at early morn, and at eventide tints with crimson and gold the clouds in the western horizon, and through the livelong day bathes the world in rays of shimmering beauty; if the world of light which at night studs with stars like glistening spears the depths of azure, be so near the blind and yet hidden from their eyes by a mere film, may not the sun of Justice with all His divine attributes and all His eternal glory be just as near to our eyes, yet hidden by a veil no more dense? And if the sun in the

heavens and the light which it dis-
penses are the veriest commonplaces
to us, while to some men they are
wholly hidden and unknown, what
must be thought of the philosophy
which in the face of this standing
fact of the world of sense, glories in
the title of agnosticism, and has
only scorn and ridicule for those
who seek to learn what little they
may of the eternal Sun of Justice
and of Glory ?

POSTSCRIPT.

Since the foregoing analogy has been in print a seeming objection has been suggested, It is one which had already occurred to myself, but which I answered only indirectly in my argument, and for the reason that it is not an objection at all. Yet, as it has suggested itself to some, it might suggest itself to others who, while they might recognize its hollowness, might at the same time be at a loss how to answer it. The objection would be that the rule is that men see and hear, and those who are blind and deaf from birth are the exceptions. Consequently the agnostic principles would hold in the majority of cases. This I have called a seeming objection, but in reality it has no bearing whatever on the analogy. One obvious answer is, that it would be found rather an unsatisfactory process, if in order to ascertain whether our conclusions are right or wrong, we were first obliged to ascertain whether those conclusions were held by a majority or a minority. But the true answer is; certainly, the majority are born with the use of their faculties, and those born without them are the exceptions, but the question is not whether men born with the use of their faculties are in the majority

or in the minority, the rule or the exception. The question at issue is whether a so-
called philosophic principle to be used in
ascertaining knowledge of ultimate truths
is sound or unsound. A sound philosohic
principle does not admit of exceptions. It
is overthrown and collapses completely
when it is shown that it admits of exceptions, and that it does not hold good in every
case in which it can be applied. A philosophical truth is like a mathematical truth
a principle in metaphysics must be as sound
as a principle in physics. If a single instance
can be adduced where it does not hold good
the so-called truth or principle falls to the
ground. If any where in the universe it
could be shown, that two and two do not
make four, but make three or five, there
would be an end to mathematical truth in
that direction. If an instance or two could
be adduced where two parallel lines come
to a point, where two straight lines form a
square, a circle or a triangle, or where the
three angles of a triangle are subtended by
~~arcs~~ *sides* measuring more or less than 180 degrees
men could not rely with certainty on the
propositions that parallel lines never meet,
that two straight lines cannot enclose a
space, or that the three angles of every triangle are equal to two right angles, and

consequently could never be sure about the truth of calculations based on these principles. If it could be shown in physics, for instance, that when the air in a bottle had been exhausted by the use of the air-pump, the air did not again rush back, but the bottle remained absolutely empty, although all obstructions had been removed, it would render uncertain the principle that nature abhors a vacuum. And precisely in the same way when in philosophy an agnostic principle is laid down; that the limitation of our faculties should be the limit line of our beliefs, and that all outside this limitation should be treated as "pure fiction" all that is necessary to overthrow the principle as false is to show an instance or two in which it will work wrong results and end in absurdities. And this I have shown to be the case in not one but in numberless instances, even in whole classes. If a principle leads us sometimes to right, sometimes to wrong conclusions, it is not a safe one to follow. And the agnostics have yet to show that this principle will lead to right conclusions. Indeed it would be easy to turn the argument against the agnostics, by simply saying that in all known cases of limitation of the faculties, as in the case of the blind and deaf, etc., from birth, the rule is not to make the limit line of credibility co-incident with the limit line of the faculties, and when the agnostics frame such a rule in the case of the Unknowable, they introduce an exception and do so without warrant and discriminate against Christian truths without giving a reason to justify them in making an exception in the case.

To return, however, to the supposed objection. Whether in cases in which the principle works absurd and ridiculous results are in the majority or in the minority has nothing whatever to do with the question. The question is the attainment of ultimate truth by right reasoning, and for this a principle must always give true results. And if I should give to a man born blind as the right rule of his belief a principle from which he must never deviate, viz. ; that he must never exceed the limits of his faculties, and I should then ask him to believe me when I told him that I saw the stars twinkle in the belt of Orion, or that I could count the exact number of stars in the Pleiades, or that Jupiter was fully as brilliant as the new moon's disc, how will he reconcile my principles with my demands on his credibility? There is a conflict between them. It matters not that I know

the truth of my remarks about the heavens,
or that all the world besides knows the
truth of them. He cannot follow the principle I have given him and at the same time
take my word for the truth of my state-
ments, for there is warfare between them.
A principle for the ascertaining of truth
should be just as good for the blind-born or
deaf-born as for the man who has the full
and perfect use of his eyes and ears, and if it
is not, it cannot be a safe or a sound one to
follow. The mental processes of the former
are not different from those of other men.
If the agnostic principle in the hands of the
former leads to absurdities, there is only
left to the agnostic to draw up one set of
principles for men with the full use of their
faculties, and a totally different set for men
afflicted with ante-natal deprivations; or, in
case they permit both classes to use the
same general principles, to give due and
timely warning to the latter, that the conclusions from those principles are apt to be
capricious, sometimes leading to truth,
sometimes to error, and that they themselves must be the judges whether those
conclusions happen to be right or wrong.
It will be easily seen, therefore, that
the objection mentioned is not in reality
an objection at all. Indeed, the analogy seems to be incontrovertible. Not

Paley's illustration of the watch, not
Butler's analogy against the Deists of
the eighteenth century was more
perfect of its kind, or more applicable to the
situation. This is by no means saying that
there is any special acumen to be credited
to the use and application to it. That it is
so apposite is due rather to the shallowness
of the new school of philosophy which
leaves itself open to such obvious objections.
The wonder to the writer has long been that
some one with a name has not long since
shown the hollowness and shallowness of
the modern school. Possibly the reason is
that no one has considered the game worth
the powder, and that I have altogether over-
estimated the importance of the agnostic.

OCTAVE OF THE FEAST OF THE IMMACULATE
  CONCEPTION,
          December 15th, 1889.

www.ingramcontent.com/pod-product-compliance
Lightning Source LLC
Chambersburg PA
CBHW021522270326
41930CB00008B/1053

* 9 7 8 3 3 3 7 2 2 1 8 0 5 *